For all the children of the world –

may the love of trees and nature show you the way

I'd like to introduce you to a dear old friend I know.
It lives out in our garden during sunshine, rain and snow.
I'll offer you a little clue to guess just what it is:
When wind is blowing through its limbs,
I swear I hear it hiss.

What's that? You need another clue to help you take a guess?
In fall it drops its leaves and makes the garden look a mess.
It's magical and colourful in summer, fall and spring.
It's something I appreciate much more than anything.

Well, that was fast! Yes, you are right; the answer is a
tree!

I'll tell you why I love it so. Please listen carefully.
It's magical – when we breathe out, the tree is breathing in.
Converting breath to oxygen, with power from within.

Communicating through their roots, the trees can say

"Hello"

and share the nutrients they need to help each other grow.
Without the trees, the weather could be dangerous and strange.
They help protect our planet from unfriendly climate change.

Trees also give us wood to make all kinds of useful things:
The homes we live in, cool new books, and children's wooden swings.
Some trees have nuts or other treats like

fig, pear and **cherry.**

They make us grow so big and strong, making us feel merry.

Our trees are not just useful; they can also be great
FUN!

I love to swing on branches in the warmth of summer sun.
Perhaps I'll build a treehouse and watch wildlife all around.
I might spy deer or foxes, as the birds sing out their sounds.

Some trees live for a **HUNDRED** years,
some trees for even more.

But all of them hide stories full of
MAGIC, love and war.

One story says a tree was prized in 1651,
for helping out a two-time king when he was on the run.
The Civil War was lost, but Charles the Second slipped away.
When captors came, he hid inside the Royal Oak all day.

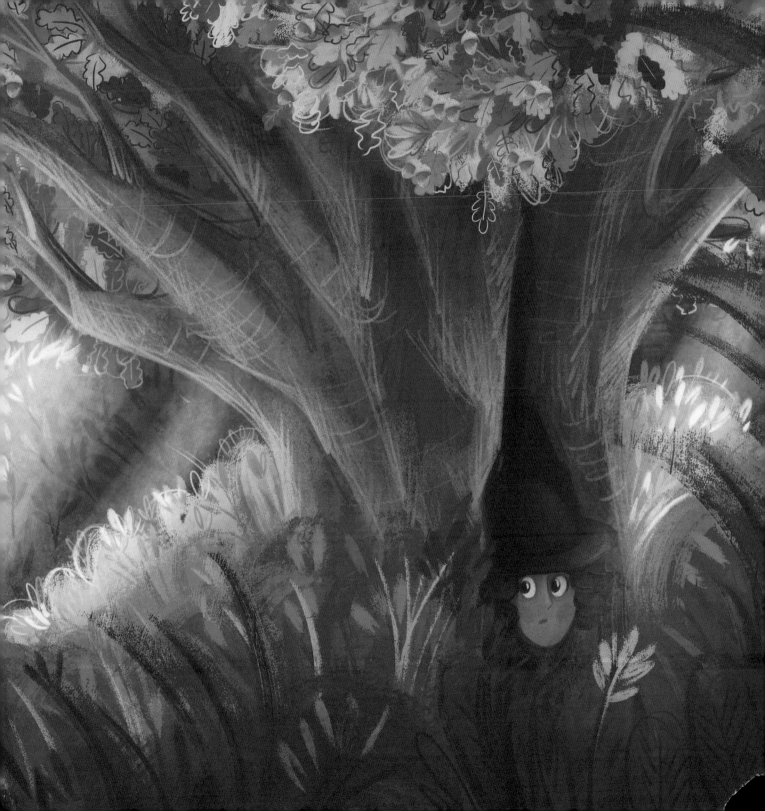

In recent years I've noticed we cut more trees than we need.
It's not too late to fix it, but it's time to

plant the seed!

I love to plant new trees with all my friends who come around.
We dig the holes together and place saplings in the ground.

The little trees need water every day to help them grow.
Their branches reach up high because of thirsty roots below.
If we all show the beauty and importance of the trees,

then we can make a difference – really!

It will be a breeze.

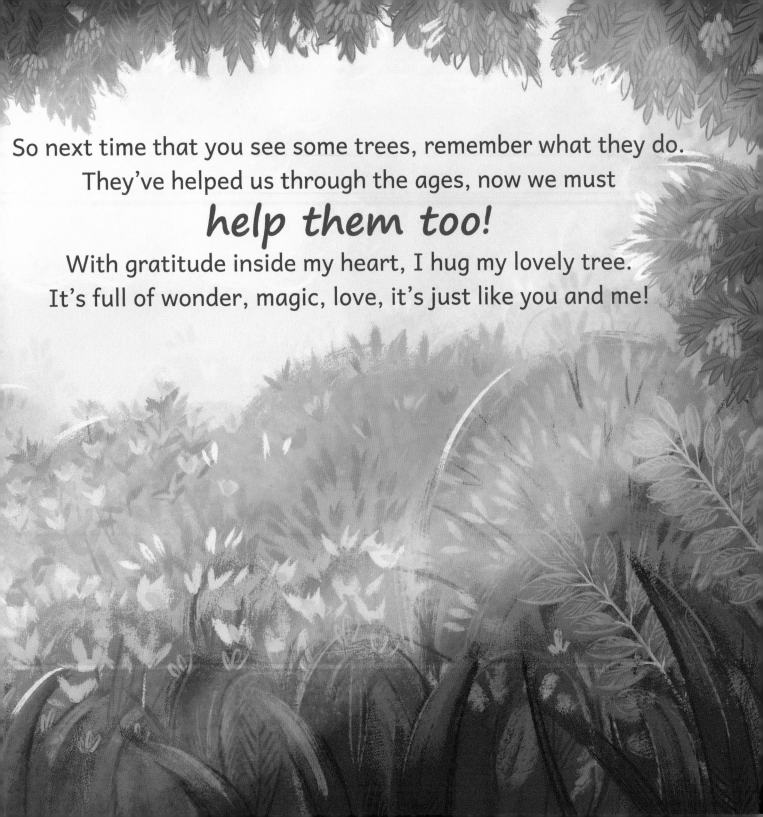

So next time that you see some trees, remember what they do.
They've helped us through the ages, now we must

help them too!

With gratitude inside my heart, I hug my lovely tree.
It's full of wonder, magic, love, it's just like you and me!

Can you spot the tree?

There are twelve trees in this book. Can you find and name them all?

Apple

Silver Birch

Maple

Horse chestnut

Linden

Oak

Beech

Fig

Pear

Rowan

Ash

Willow

How can we help?

Every year we cut between 3.5 billion to 7 billion trees. Here are five ways you can protect the trees every day:

1.  Recycle paper – when you finish with paper make sure you put it in the recycling bin.

2.  Reuse paper – draw on both sides of the paper, use scrap paper, make toys from cardboard, empty toilet paper or kitchen towels. You can use them for building castles, cars, forts, or wherever your imagination will take you.

3.  Borrow, share and donate books – you don't have to buy a new book, you can buy a second-hand book or borrow it from a library. If you get a new book, share it or donate it when it's not needed anymore.

4.  Love trees and nature – go for a walk in the forest, hug the trees, notice all the wildlife around them, feel the connection with trees when you breathe. Have you noticed different trees smell differently? Have you noticed the difference in the air in the forest and the air in the town/city? Fall in love with trees and nature and you will become a Protector of Trees.

5.  Plant a tree – there are many organisations helping children to plant trees. Find one in your local area to make sure the right time and the right tree is chosen.

Other books by the author:

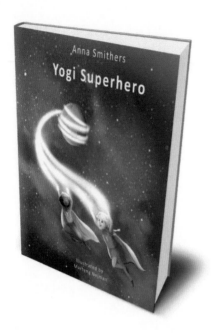  

Dear adult – Thank you for reading this book! If you enjoyed it, please consider leaving a review. It would mean the world to me! Thank you.

Hi children – I love receiving letters, drawings and pictures. Feel free to email anna@annasmithers.com and I will try my best to email you back!

A. Smithers

Printed in Great Britain
by Amazon

Tree Full of Wonder

Anna Smithers

7000000397033

Text © Anna Smithers 2021

Illustrations © Martyna Nejman 2021

Book design by Victoria Smith

Orange Lotus Publishing

www.annasmithers.com

ISBN 978-1-8383391-4-2 - paperback

ISBN 978-1-8383391-5-9 – hardcover